Broken For Better

Shar Vegas Moore

Alpha Publishing.

Dedication

"Broken for Better" is dedicated to readers who find themselves lost in trauma. In the midst of pain, it's hard to find your way out of a place you've never been. Sometimes, we have support, and sometimes, we are too ashamed or too lost to ask for help. I wrote these words to encourage you to keep the faith. Understand that trauma, pain, and confusion are sometimes a part of the process. It is my hope that the contents of this book will inspire you to stay in the process of "becoming." Becoming who you are destined to be happens in stages. Whether you are at the stage of acknowledgment, addressing it, or embracing it, this book will help guide you through. I extend my dedication to my therapist, Felicia Reid, who helped me walk through darkness to recognize my light. Furthermore, I wish to also dedicate these words to those who have suffered emotional abuse and are struggling to find the light in the midst of healing. Self awareness and self love is the key to wholeness. It is also the key to giving and receiving love from others. I am especially grateful for my family and friends, that were supportive through my healing journey and help me keep the faith. Thank you for your support. May God continue to bless you and cover your journey.

Contents

Introduction

For so long, I walked in darkness, trying to be a light. I spent years of my life trying to heal and inspire others. Instead, I continued to lose my own way. It never occurred to me that I, too, was lost. Derived from a Christian background, I grew up with the importance of God and church being drilled into my brain. I always knew the value of acknowledging God, but I was passive in my awareness. Life brought about many challenges and changes. Each stage, I maneuvered, without stopping to take account of my last journey. Unknowingly, trauma and pain began to accumulate in my life. I experienced disappointment after disappointment, heartbreak after heartbreak. Some, I caused on myself.

My childhood immolated the importance of faith, but my adulthood rarely demonstrated it. I grew up in low-income, poverty-stricken neighborhoods where dreaming was just that. My family spoke of God and went to church, but in rare instances, I witnessed them truly walk in the grace and favor of God. I witnessed drug abuse in my home and in my community. Domestic violence among my extended family members was prevalent. These atrocities were normalities in my environment. My guardians and parents taught me that being strong meant to keep going. Many situations and childhood traumas were unaddressed. At that time, I did not understand the value of healing, therapy, and truly having faith in God. I can honestly say, no one in my environment appeared to either. Something on the inside of me still knew I had to be better.

I desired from a young child to be great. From elementary school, up until college, I chased greatness. Many days, I came home from school to a house with no lights nor water. My mom and aunt would get crackheads in the community to illegally turn the lights and water back on. This lasted for some time, but not long. I became accustomed to lack. My mom raised me and my sibling in Section 8 housing. In this, we always had a place to stay, but other necessities like food, water, and sometimes lights were a privilege. The food stamps we received from the government were sometimes exchanged for rent money. I watched my mother and my aunt fiercely try to provide by working day and night. As they would say, "robbing Peter to pay Paul." This phrase meant that one need had to be sacrificed in order to meet another need. This was a normal sacrifice in my home. Though it sounds displaced and troubling, I thank God for each and every experience.

The desolation and lack of life fueled my ambition to run after grace and abundance. I knew I deserved better. Each challenge and stage taught me something new. I did not always get the lesson in the midst of the trouble. When I look back and see how far God has brought me, I am grateful. My mom always said, "Life could be worse". She was right. I took this perspective, and, for the most part, excelled in it. Of course, this was before adulthood and bills and failed relationships. The few lessons and lack of structure in my childhood only took me so far. The prayers of my grandmother and mother shield me through my childhood. Once I became an adult, life showed me I needed my own courage and relationship with God. I began to pray and ask God for my own awareness and truth of who he was in my life. In some seasons, he showed up immediately. In others, I felt like he was not there at all. In my awareness, I knew better. Each stage challenged my understanding of how God works and what a true relationship with him meant. My perspective on life began to change. In doing so, I found peace and courage to write these words. Each excerpt shares a different experience and a new awareness that came from each.

Chapter 1
Acknowledge It

The first step to solving any problem is to recognize the problem exists. For some, that problem may be addiction, self-doubt, or even self-sabotaging. For me, it was trauma. My trauma caused me to relive cycles by perceiving the circumstance or the person incorrectly. Understanding and accepting reality is important. Being an optimist can sometimes be detrimental when you are avoiding the truth. This was my problem. I had to accept this in order to change it. I had to reflect on recurring events and episodes through my relationships in order to develop a plan for change. When there have been multiple traumatic experiences and maladaptive behaviors in place, reflecting and acceptance are easier said than done. Trauma has many forms and definitions. Webster defines trauma as "a deeply distressing or disturbing experience". That experience can be mental, physical, emotional, or all three. Trauma impacts a person's response as well as their mental and emotional state. Depending on the severity, the after effects of trauma can last for a few days or several decades. The degree of impact trauma has on a person depends on varying factors. These factors include his/her mental capacity prior to the traumatic event, programmed responses, support or lack thereof, and culture.

Some people are referred to as "stronger" than others.

Contrarily, all persons are equally weak when they are not surrounded by the right support and equipped with the emotional intelligence on how to heal. A healthy support system, such as family members and friends, positively impacts healing. Going through a traumatic experience and not being interrelated or feeling a sense of belonging, has a negative impact on a traumatic experience. This chapter highlights my real-life experiences that helped me realize and accept my trauma. It gives first-person accounts of my thoughts and feelings during my moments of joy and despair. Although my experiences would have been less traumatic with a stronger support system, I am thankful to God I had a support system at all. Without God and my immediate family, my realization would have kept me in a dark, depressive state.

Rich and Homeless

"Vegas to the topside? Vegas to the topside", the DJ repeated. A tall, fair-skinned female seductively made her way to the stage. Flickers of her platform shoes gracefully floated through the clouds of smoke. The DJ played a slow, seductive song as she began to make love to the pole. Guys crowded around, throwing wrinkled dollar bills. She began to climb the pole. I watched in amazement. She hung upside down like a monkey, half-naked and gorgeous. Money covered the dance floor as she continued to mesmerize the audience. I couldn't believe it. I was watching my girlfriend dance for money. We had been dating for over 2 years, and I had never witnessed her so alive and entertaining. She continued to dance as the songs changed. After three songs, she exited the stage. 5 a.m. came fast. "You ready, bae?" she asked. "Yeah, let's go. Aj is with Ashley", I replied.

AJ was her 3-year-old son we were raising together. Ashley was her best friend who babysat while we worked or needed time alone. I worked at the local grocery store in Aventura, Miami. Moments later, a yellow cab pulled up to the "Foxy Lady" nightclub and picked us up. It was her routine to catch cabs after work. We had a regular cab driver pick her up each night. "20, 40, 60, 80….." I heard her say. I laid in our bed listening to her count the tips she made. Each night, she would come home after dancing and sit on the toilet in our stall-size bathroom counting ones. The grocery store only paid me $9 per hour, hardly enough to keep food on our table. I worked so she did not feel alone in trying to provide for our family and so I did not feel worthless. Most nights, she made $400-$1000 in tips. On a good night, she brought home $1500. Smelling like long-island ice tea and incredible hulks, she climbed into the bed beside me and went fast asleep. The next morning, I caught the city bus to Ashley's to go pick up AJ. "C'mon AJ," I yelled while pulling him to walk faster so we didn't miss the bus. Our routine was to go shopping for the house and pay bills while she slept for her shift later that night. In Miami, the strip clubs opened at 12:00 noon.

When we really needed money, she went to work in the afternoons. The lawyers, doctors, and police officers normally snuck into the strip clubs at midday to keep the secret from getting home to their wives. I went to the local grocery store and, cashed in the one-dollar bills, and did the normal shopping. The Winn Dixie was in the shopping plaza two blocks down on NW 57th Avenue, 1 mile away. Aj and I normally walked there, considering we did not have a car. We purchased groceries and oftentimes spent 50% of the money she earned the night before on new outfits. My partner made money so fast, that saving was the last thing on our minds. As fast as she made the money, we spent it. Her grandma and mother hated me. In their perception, I was her pimp. I, too, knew she was intelligent and had more potential and ambition than being a dancer. However, it was something she did before I met her. It was not my job to change her mind. I accepted her decision, and in all honesty, the money she was making was more than most people with a Master's Degree.

I was finishing my shift at work when my phone rang. We were not allowed to be on cell phones at work, so, I did not answer. My phone continued to ring. Finally, logging off my cash register, I answered. "Hello!" I yelled, concerned. "Bae!" my partner on the other end confirmed anxiously. I could tell something was wrong. "Yea!", I responded. "Our roof has collapsed," she exclaimed. I wanted to be sure I heard her correctly. "The roof what!" I asked. "The roof on the house is wide open." I ran to the time clock, barely explaining to my supervisor I had to go. I jogged to the bus stop almost a mile away from my job just in time to catch the overcrowded #3 Biscayne Blvd route. Per usual, people were standing shoulder to shoulder, hanging on to any piece of exposed grab bar. We were so close, that you could feel the person standing next to you breathing. The city bus looked like a clear representation of America; every culture, gender, and generation was all packed into one bus. It sounded like a beehive, with several conversations in different languages all occurring at once.

I quickly grabbed a piece of the overhead metal bar as the driver slammed the door and raced down Biscayne Blvd. When I arrived home, AJ and my partner were sitting in the living room. I went into our bedroom, hoping my partner was pranking me. A hole the size of two watermelons was positioned directly over our bed. Pieces of shingles and drywall were scattered over the bed sheets. I was speechless. "What are we going to do?" my partner asked with tears in her eyes. She and AJ looked to me for security, decision-making, and protection. "I don't know," I replied ashamedly. We were renting an in-law quarters from a high-school classmate of hers. It was small but affordable. Considering she knew our landlord from childhood, we did not have a rental contract. It was just somewhere we stayed for cheap because my wages did not allow us to rent elsewhere. Her wages were non-verifiable and, therefore, could not be used on rental applications to get us approved elsewhere. I flopped down on the couch with no words in mind. Reaching over to hug my partner, I whispered, "We will be okay." I felt her shoulders relax. Truth be told, I had no clue what we were going to do. Here we were with a three year old, a collapsing roof, and not a penny saved.

At that moment, every bad financial decision we ever made came running back to us. For months, we had been spending $200-$500 per day, blowing money carelessly. We shopped and ate take out everyday, not thinking about emergencies. We had no financial discipline. I finally responded, "We cannot stay here". "Let's pack some clothes and head to a hotel. That night, we stayed in "The Shalimar," a local hotel that gave an illusion of being a fancy hotel but honestly was a hiding place for prostitutes and drug dealers. The hotel was right off Biscayne, surrounded by rich and fancy hotels. We stayed in the hotel for weeks, still unable to save. She continued to go to work each night, but now out of desperation. We all slept in the full-size bed and most days ate off the same plate. Each night she went to work, AJ and I stayed in the hotel room. Several nights passed, and my partner barely brought home $200. We could barely afford the nightly hotel rate and food. We reached out to family members who, too, had money problems and could not help. Eventually, we were down to our last $32. "I tell you what, y'all stay in the park and play all day until I go to work and make some money for tonight," my partner bargained. She knew my strength was weakening with not being able to save my family.

The night began to fall, and still, there was no sign of my partner. We had been waiting in the park for almost 8 hours. I began to worry. It was getting pitch black, and everyone had gone home. AJ and I sat on the park bench. It was almost 10 p.m. Moments later, my partner came walking through the darkness, almost in slow motion. I could tell she had been crying. "What's wrong?" I asked while holding AJ in my arms. He was sound asleep. "I didn't make enough money," she wept. She almost fell to her knees, but instead into my chest. I placed my arms around her, and we cried. It was at that moment we realized we were homeless. We sat and cried in silence without a word to say. Several hours passed. "Hold AJ," I requested. I took my jacket off and laid it across the bench. I then laid down and instructed her to lay on top of my body. I was so ashamed. I didn't have a place for my family to sleep. Because we were homosexuals, her family refused to help us, and my family was over 1,000 miles away. I laid on the bench, so she and our son could lie on top of my body and not have to sleep on the hard bench. Tears rolled down my face as I stared up at the sky. Aj was still sound asleep with not a care in the world. My partner clinched me and our son at the same time, drained and weak.

After laying there for several hours, my body became stiff. I knew we would not last through the night. I woke my partner up on my chest. "I know you don't want to hear this, but you have to go to your family's house," I stated. "No!" she rebutted. Her eyes began to tear up. I knew in her heart she viewed this as betrayal of our union. She also knew that I would be left alone in the streets and that she and our son were the only reason I was in Miami. I could tell she felt it was her fault.

"Listen, we have Aj. We cannot stay out here," I tried to convince her. She sat upright with Aj in her arms, crying. I noticed a police officer sitting over in the parking lot. It was pitch black, and therefore, he did not notice us sleeping on the bench. "Imma go ask the officer to give us a ride to a shelter," I suggested. "I am not going to a shelter in Vegas" my partner replied, crying. "It's our only option," I demanded. I walked through the darkness towards the police car; tapping the window. "Excuse me officer" I beggared timidly. He was startled and rolled down the window. "Where did you come from?" he asked. "My partner and our son were here all along sleeping on the bench back there," I confirmed. He looked through his rear view mirror to confirm what I was saying. "Why are you all out here?" he asked with confusion on his face. "Well, our roof collapsed in our home. We then stayed in a hotel for several weeks and finally ran out of funds. We did not have enough money to pay for another night." I explained. "Can you take us to a shelter?" I asked. "Do you not have any family?" the officer asked. "My family is far away and her family is not happy that we are living a homosexual lifestyle and refuses to affiliate with her as long as she is with me." I explained.

The officer sat with his mouth open, stunned. "Also, if you take us to a shelter, can you please keep this a secret?" I requested. "A secret? Why?" he asked. "Well her mother is probably your co-worker. She has been working for the Miami Police Department for over 20 years," I continued. I could tell he was mind blown. "My partner doesn't want her mother to know and that's why she is refusing to go to a shelter and does not want me to come talk to you." I continued. I could see the disappointment in his eyes. "Get your things and y'all c'mon," he demanded. I walked back and told my partner to c'mon. She was pissed but knew it was too late to not follow through. She also realized I had my mind made up and the only thing she could do was leave me or go with the plan. I was desperate and concerned about our son's safety. We both knew the risk of us being ostracized and possibly even separated, but I had to do something. We got into the back of the police car. The officer was calling several shelters in the area; none had beds for that night. "Ladies, I'll take you all to get something to eat, then pay for your hotel for tonight. Tomorrow we can work on getting you a bed at the local shelter." he explained. That night we slept in the hotel. I remember holding both our son and my partner closer than I ever did. The morning came. The local shelter sent a van to pick us up from the hotel. The van arrived around 11:30 a.m. close to time for us to check out. It was two black men. "Hey, are you the family that needs a place to stay?" the driver asked. Both men looked as if they just got hired that day and possibly were homeless themselves. Me and my partner locked eyes. "Yes!" I replied. "Okay. Gather your things, we are here to take you to the shelter." At that moment, our lives and our relationship began to change.

The first 24 hours at the shelter were a cultural shock. The driver from the van sorted through all of our personal items as if we were turning ourselves in for jail. "You can't take any electronics, nor that laptop in the shelter," he demanded. "So what are we supposed to do with it?" my partner sarcastically asked. "I don't know, but you can't take it with us," he answered. I looked at my partner with compassion and, took the laptop, and threw it in the trash. "I'll get us another one," I comforted her. We didn't understand. It was like we were being stripped of the only things we had, just to go into a shelter and have a place to stay. "Those bags of clothes you have are also too big. You will only have a 5-inch by 5-inch locker in the shelter. Anything that cannot fit in that locker will have to be placed in storage or thrown away." The man continued. We were stumped and speechless. My partner looked at me with concern and also the "I told you this was a bad idea" face.

I tried to remain positive. "Just keep all AJ's clothes and the things you want. I can get me some more clothes." I suggested. We stood in the hotel parking lot outside of the running van, sorting through clothes. Before we could get in the van, we threw away half of our belongings. The last little dignity we had left was stripped from us. We rode silently in the van to the shelter. It was a shock all over me and my partner's face. Reality was sitting in. I knew my partner was not stable in her emotions. I sucked up every ounce of despair and tapped into my survival mode. When we arrived at the shelter in downtown Overtown in the city of Miami, there were bob wires and gates around the shelter like a prison. People were crowded around the outside of the facility, smoking cigarettes and hanging out as if it was a party. They all watched as we unloaded and walked through the gates. We had no clue what we were about to experience.

What we thought was a safe place was a walk through hell. As we entered the shelter, they checked the few belongings we were allowed to bring, searched us for weapons, and sat us in a waiting room to be assigned to a caseworker. I could see the fear in my partner's eyes. "Ms. Cason," a Hispanic lady appeared and called out. My partner turned to see who she was. "I am your caseworker," she explained as she extended her hand. "You and your son can come with me," she continued. "What about my girlfriend?" my partner asked. "She will have her own case worker," the lady replied. In that instant, what we feared the most was definite. The shelter was going to separate us due to us being homosexuals and not recognized as a family. Not to mention, we were not married. I watched my partner and our son walk down the hall. My heart dropped. Resentment entered into my heart. Later that day, we were assigned to different quarters. My partner was assigned to the single mother quarters with our son, and I was sent to the single women's quarters with other single women. My quarters had over 75 women lying on bunk beds with a small metal locker at the end of each. The lockers were the size of a kids' shoe box. Very few beds had blankets, only sheets. The other women watched as I unpacked my grocery bag of belongings and placed them in the locker. They could sense I had no business being in the shelter. They could also sense I was still in shock, and at any moment, I could lose my cool, so they had no interest in making conversation. They just watched. Here I was, 22 years old with a Bachelor's Degree, unpacking a grocery bag to sleep in a shelter. I knew of a God, I believed in a God, but at that moment, I had no clue where he was. That night, I laid on top of my bed, unable to close my eyes. All I could think about was my partner and our son.

Most importantly, I pondered on a way to get us out of there. "Lights out!" a lady came walking down the aisles of the quarter. She had a key to unlock the light switch and cut off every light except the bathroom area. It was about 10:00 p.m. I laid still, listening to the different breathing patterns of the other women in the quarters. What felt like moments later, I heard staff coming around. "Everybody up!" the staff yelled. I reached into my pants and grabbed my phone to see what time it was. It was 5:30 a.m. That explained why the bums were always out and about so early. The shelters woke everyone up around 5:30 a.m.

We had to be out of the quarters by 7:30 a.m. each morning. For the first few mornings, this did not bother me. I was anxious to see my family, and I could only see them if we met up in the common areas like the playground. When it was time for breakfast, we stood outside in a line, waiting for a seat to become available in the small cafeteria. My partner and I were yet again heartbroken. The families and single mothers ate first and, therefore rarely were allowed to eat with the single men and women. I stood in the line with the single women, looking through the cafeteria glass at my family eating without me. I had no idea the trauma I was experiencing. It was the hardest thing I had done that far in life, but after several days, we began to adapt. My partner would hurry up and eat so I could get inside the cafeteria and eat while she waited in the common area for me to come out. Other days, she and I didn't eat at all. We saved the little money I had from working at the grocery store to buy AJ food, and we all sat in the common areas together during dinner time. That was the only time we had to spend together while inside the shelter. Otherside, we would leave and meet up outside the shelter at the train station or on the bench outside the shelter. The other homeless people recognized we were inseparable and in love. They felt bad for us and the treatment we were receiving. Many of them helped us sneak notes to eat other, or helped us sneak and see each other while inside the shelter. It was hard to recognize the difference between being in the shelter and being incarcerated.

And the Wig Comes Off

I remember putting on my pants, brushing my teeth, and washing my face. Life was, yet again, doing what life does. I had fallen in love with my cheerleader peer from middle school. We attended middle school and high school together. She was gorgeous and gracious. We also lived in the same neighborhood, but her mother never allowed her to ride the school bus or play outside. Every middle school and high school game, we were around each other. I played basketball and volleyball, and she cheered.

I never viewed her in a romantic light. I truly was never attracted to her. When she first reached out to me, I couldn't believe it. I never thought I had a chance, in fact, I never considered it. For over 10 years, I had not spoken to nor seen her. I graduated high school and left immediately after college. I lived away from my hometown for 8 years. Funny how life works. The only time I had considered her in the past, was to embarrass a less athletic cheerleader in a cheer-off. She reached out to me on social media after I, jokingly, commented on how gorgeous she looked under one of her Facebook pictures. I didn't think anything of it. I was witty and always making jokes under everyone's pictures.

"Hey, with yo lil sexy bald head," I commented.

Indeed, it was not the most romantic statement, but I knew she was aware of my joking personality and would not take it personally.

In fact, I did not expect a reply at all. Days later, I checked my inbox and realized she had messaged me.

"Hey, how have you been?" she asked.

"I am well", I replied.

"Why did you comment on my page?" she asked.

"You posted a picture. I make comments on everyone's pictures," I replied.

We continued to chat. She made me aware that she had a 4-year-old little girl and was still living in our hometown, Columbia, S.C. That first conversation, we chatted for hours. She shared with me her career path as a cosmetologist and also working full-time for the state.

I enjoyed her conversation, but had no intent on it being anything more. "You like women?" I asked sarcastically.

"I have had sexual encounters with women and enjoyed it, but I have never dated a woman," she replied. "I have a boyfriend," she continued. I was not surprised by her reply. What I was concerned about was how she had so much time on her hands to entertain my conversation when I was openly a lesbian. She began to explain how her dating life was complicated. She was dating a married man with three children; who allegedly was separated and anticipating a divorce. We began to talk more and more each day. Each day, the conversations became intense and more personal. I still had no clue of what her true intentions were but we could not seem to stop talking to each other. We video chat with each other 3 and sometimes 4 times a day, each time for several hours long. Most times just staring into each other's eyes in silence.

At first, I believed it to just be platonic. I considered she viewed it as something to do to pass the time, since her man did not seem to have time for her. More and more, we grew attached to each other. Before I knew it, 2 months had passed by. "I cannot continue to talk with you in a relationship," I mentioned. "Well, I'm not technically in a relationship," she rebutted. "It's more like a situation where I am seeing a married man who claims to be separated from his wife. They have kids together, and he cannot seem to completely separate his relationship with his kids from his relationship with her," she added. "Well, whatever it is you and him have, I don't want to come between that," I urged. "I would rather talk with you when you are completely available." I contested. She did not like this idea, but respected it. We ceased our chatting and online flirting for about two months. Not long after, she was back in my inbox.

We picked up where we left off and began to fall in love. Our relationship was long distance. She lived in Columbia, SC, and I lived in Charlotte, NC. I traveled twice a week to close the gap in our hearts. She sometimes came to my house in Charlotte to visit and spend the weekend. Considering she had never lived a lesbian lifestyle, I could not stay in her home. The days I did go over to her house, I pretended to be a client getting my hair done. Indeed, I did need my hair groomed, but most times, I could care less. Her mom and father lived next door and very much scrutinized her life. She rented the next-door mobile home her parents placed on the same property when she was younger. Each morning, her mother came over at 6:00 a.m. with a spare key. I found this to be alarming, considering she was 32 years old. "Does your mom come over every morning?" I asked. "Yes." She replied. "She comes over to see my daughter get on the school bus," she attempted to explain. "How so? She lives right across the grass and can simply see her off from the porch?" I questioned. I quickly learned her mother controlled most of her social life and her daughter's too. Any company she had over to her house, her mom called her phone to verify, if not walked over. I stayed my distance to keep the peace in her family. We enjoyed each other's company.

Night after night, we fell asleep on the phone together. It became a normal thing. Her daughter began to speak to me and get attached just by us being on the phone so often. Even her best friends became accustomed to us talking and not before long had figured out it was more to us than just braids. For a year and a half, we played the part. She kept the secret from her mom, dad, and sister, and I patiently waited. We talked, traveled, and spent nights together in hotel rooms or at my house. It was not ideal or allowed for her to have overnight visitors in her own home. Her mother used the excuse that it was her property, and she had a daughter to control who came and went and her house. We were in love, and could no longer hide it. The days seemed longer when we didn't talk or when we were not able to travel to see each other. I took every off day and vacation time I could to spend with her and her daughter. At least twice a week, I was traveling to accommodate her schedule and to keep her secret intact. After all, I had been living an open gay lifestyle since a teenager and had no reason to tip-toe. Out of respect for her family as well as her process and timing, I continued to creep. Our feelings for each other became obvious. Those who were around us, could clearly see we were intimate and closer than a normal hairstylist and client. Eventually, her mom and sister found out. She was reading a book that I had gifted her when one of our photos that she was using as a bookmark fell out of the book. According to her, her mom was speechless. I'm sure you could have bought her for a penny. We were kissing in the photo; and not like cosmetologists kiss clients. It was a photo where I had surprised her and took her to a private vineyard for a wine tasting in North Carolina.

The picture spoke volumes. This was the beginning of our trauma and nightmare as a couple. Her mom was a church-going Christian who looked down on everyone's sins but her own. She attended church two and sometimes three times a week. Their church was very small, so small that she and her family were the congregation and the choir members. She had been raised in that church for over 25 years and never worshiped anywhere else. It was routine for her and her sister. Now, it was routine for her daughter as well. "Listen, I don't want to come between you and your family nor your religion," I said to her. "You not", she replied. "I am not gay because of you. I have been with women before and enjoyed it, just never in a relationship," she assured me. "Yea, but I have been down this road before. This can get very ugly and demeaning for us both," I explained. "I do not want to experience that hurt of family rejection due to my lifestyle again. God and my family love and respect who I am, and therefore, I cannot tolerate an outsider telling me who I am not," I declared. Many of our conversations consisted of this. She understood but could not accept me walking away. We were in love and had fallen for each other unexpectedly. Her best friends supported us. They could see how happy she was and shared they had never seen her that happy before. She, too, knew this but understood that she would have to separate from her parents and all that she had ever known for us to truly be happy.

After almost two years of hurting, feeling isolated, and desolate, she decided to move away from her parents. She prepared a letter to her mom and grandmother confirming all the rumors of her and I as a couple. Confronting her fears of them knowing and bashing us with the Bible, did not stop them. Each week, they created a different emotional obstacle with their judgment. We had no true issues of our own. Some days, when I called her, I could hear her depressed tone. "I'm ready to get away from here," she would cry as if trapped in a dungeon. It hurt my soul. I knew that she was stuck between happiness and a new life, and letting go of all she had ever known. We both knew this was the hardest decision she ever had to make. I did not want that for her. She did not want me to feel responsible for her having to make a choice. Her mother and grandmother made indirect comments like "Be careful," as if I was going to hurt her or her child in some way. She even went so far as to tell her that I was no longer allowed on the property, even to truly get my hair down or sit outside in my car. It was a nightmare and weighed down our happiness.

Day in and day out, I listened to her cry, wanting to be happy but not having the courage to decide. Because my heart raced like a stallion at the track when I saw her, I waited. Her daughter and I had developed our own connection and relationship. She, too, loved to see me coming and hated to see me go. She said things like, "Mama, let's go live with Shar-Shar." That was her way of saying, let's be a family. We both brushed the comments off as if not to hear them, knowing we wanted the same thing. It was hard, one of the hardest things I ever persevered through. It was like the love of my life was in jail and denied bond. It was also frustrating, because I knew I had enough love and protection for the both of us. Considering she had never been protected by a love other than her parents, she knew this but had trouble accepting it. I had a three-bedroom home where I lived alone with my dog, so stability was not an issue. I also knew that it would take her some time to accept that she was now living in another world. She had no clue what she got herself into, and had no idea nor desire to get out.

Finally, I got what I had been waiting for and most certainly wanted. We moved in together in Charlotte, NC. It felt good to be a happy family. Moving together was something the three of us wanted; me, my partner, and her daughter. I grew up in a home with one parent, so fostering an environment of love and happiness made me happy. It was my desire to provide them with everything they needed. Anxiety and self-sabotaging thoughts still threatened me about not being enough, but I made a conscious effort to fight off the thoughts and doubts of the outsiders.

My partner and I moved into a two-bedroom upscale apartment in the Southend of Charlotte, NC. The rent was excessive and overpriced, but the property was beautiful, and I vowed to make sure she and her daughter lived comfortably. Like the dominant role, I managed to take care of the major bills in our home. I personally decorated our home, each room with elegance and character to make them feel comfortable. The times were great. My partner's responsibility was to take care of nurturing our home. In doing so, she cooked, did the laundry, and offered any emotional support me and our daughter needed. She still worked, but only for her own pleasures. She was a workaholic, so asking her to completely stop working was out of the question. I didn't mind her working. I wanted her to feel valued and have self fulfillment. I figured, as long as I paid the bills, and helped her in being happy with herself, us being happy, together, would have longevity.

My job paid well but was horrible. I had no set schedule. Some days, I was required to be at work at 5:00 a.m., while other nights, I worked until almost midnight. My off days were never the same. Luckily, my partner had a set schedule. She worked from 8:00 a.m.-4:30 p.m. daily with every weekend off. She was always off on holidays and able to spend time with our daughter and her family. She was even allowed to work from home. I couldn't say the same. I had to work to maintain the life I so badly wanted to provide for her and our daughter.

On Thursdays, no matter how tired I was, I managed to make it date night. I loved seeing her smile, and taking her out to show her my work did not make me lose sight of what it was all about. When I got off at 3:00 p.m., I picked our daughter up from school and took her to the park. My life, in my perspective, was a dream come true. Soon, life taught me, perspective is everything. We had been living together for 6 months when I noticed my partner's attentiveness and awareness began to fade. She had recently picked up a new part-time job at a hair store to align with her goals of opening a hair salon. In my perspective, she didn't need the money. From her perspective, she was in debt. I agreed to the idea, hoping that this would get her closer to her dreams and self-fulfillment. I had no clue that it would cost us our happiness together. After all, I worked and paid all the bills so that she would have the autonomy to chase whatever dreams she had. I was excited but also nervous for her. I knew that my partner's never-ending desire to make money would soon catch up to her, catch up to us. I held these thoughts to myself.

She began working 6 days a week, between two jobs. I would work all day and come home to neither her nor our daughter's home. Breakfast, nor dinner was no longer available, and most times, I had no clue where she was. I resisted the urge to snoop and be the controlling partner, so I continued life as if nothing was wrong, hoping she would notice her own neglectful ways and recalibrate. Months went by, and she became more and more absent. Eventually, we were just roommates who had occasional sex. The only time we had date night, were nights I planned. Even with planning, I still had to pay for the dates. This was the norm for our relationship. I didn't mind it, as long as my partner appreciated and demonstrated gratitude. I began to feel neglected. My partner would come home late and leave early the next day. Our schedules were completely opposite and, even worse, unknown. My mind began to wander, and all the self-sabotaging thoughts came rushing back. Never did my partner stop to notice how our relationship was suffering. Day in and day out, she was concerned about making money. I didn't understand. I paid all the bills and provided for all the major needs.

My frustration began to build inside. I was working so hard to provide for my family, and all I required was a little more gratitude for my sacrifices from my partner. I kept my feelings and thoughts inside. I didn't want to run her off with complaints, but I knew things needed to be addressed. My partner was absent and passive. If it wasn't about money or our daughter, it was the last thing on her mind. I didn't understand this. We began to grow apart. Distress began to fill my heart, and tears in my eyes. Some days, I cried after she left in the morning to take our daughter to school. I knew she didn't see what was happening to us. I almost felt like she didn't care to see. For several months, we went through the motions. I continued working and paying the bills, and she continued doing whatever. All the anger and frustration came spewing out.

One night, we got into a heated argument about sex. I had just returned from a bar trying to drink my feelings of missing our happy times off. I returned home to our two bedroom apartment and entered our bedroom. She was lying there as if she was asleep. I gently slid into the bed next to her, longing for her approval and touch. She mushed me off like a stray dog. All the rejection I ever felt came rushing back.

Every moment I longed to be loved, supported, touched, and coddled came rushing back. I got angered and began yelling things like "We are over" and "I'm moving out." We had become so estranged, we already tried sleeping in separate bedrooms. She jumped out of the bed as if a stranger was lying next to her. I felt so alone and neglected. I didn't understand. I never cheated nor betrayed our bond. That night, we argued and fought until 5:30 a.m. At 2:40 p.m. on June 15, 2022, she called her parents and, packed all her things and left. Everything we had fought through to stay together, everything we worked hard to maintain, and every financial and emotional sacrifice I made for us went out the window. That day, I lost my family, I lost my home, and I lost myself.

I continued going to work and doing the bare minimum things in life. I couldn't think or process anything but working and sleeping. Things like shopping and traveling, I ceased to do. My job and the scheduling didn't help much. Each day, I came home to the empty apartment where she and my daughter used to be; I was triggered. I pulled up in the parking lot each day, wishing it was all a bad dream and her car would be there. Most weeks, I worked 6 days a week. This helped numb and ignore the pain.

My laundry piled up, the dishes overflowed, and my refrigerator was empty. I felt like the walking dead. I couldn't find joy in anything. Most days, I had a pocket full of money, a nice car, a nice apartment, and a well-paying job and I still could not find a smile. I just felt numb. Hours would pass me by, and I would not even be present. I was so hurt, I did not recognize myself when I looked in the mirror. I felt like a zombie. What I didn't realize was depression was knocking down my door.

Chapter 2

Address It

In my healing journey, I created the A.A.E. method. A.A.E. is an acronym for "Acknowledge, Address, and Embrace". The hardest stage of this process was acknowledgment. Reality setting in about my true mental and emotional state did not feel good, especially coming from a background where emotions are rarely addressed. Accepting I was broken, desolate, and lost was the most painful realization I ever experienced.

Although the revelation brought a new understanding of who I was and who I needed to become, it also came with pain and disappointment about how far off I was from who I wanted to be. I came to understand, that in order to get emotionally free and relieved from the pain, I had to address what I acknowledged. Some therapists say addressing the problem is just as hard as acknowledging it. Considering my own healing journey, I cannot argue against this point. Culture, familiar status, religion, and many other factors impact how people confront their problems or trauma. Some people utilize religion and a spiritual aspect. Others, take a more practical approach and seek counseling and therapy. I learned that most of the world exercises a more popular tactic such as avoidance and fails to address their issues at all. At different stages in my healing journey, I fell in all three categories.

In my early adolescence, I was not taught to confront my emotions. My family did not discuss emotions, grief, or trauma, for that matter. In fact, it was rarely acknowledged. Coming from an oppressed lineage, only matters of necessity tended to. In my family, emotions were just feelings that we could not afford to entertain. Being raised in a Christian background, I was raised to pray about all things. There was an unspoken concept of prayer being the only answer. I embedded this concept in my early adulthood. When I experienced disappointment, lack, or pain, I prayed. Indeed, my prayers provided me with relief but only praying is what fostered an environment of avoidance. I began to learn the importance of mental health in my grad school years as a clinical mental health student.

My studies revealed the error in my coping techniques and maladaptive behaviors. I subscribed to many different coping strategies, including drug use. Some days, I smoked 3-5 blunts of marijuana. Other days, I cried in random parking lots. Most times, I avoided my pain by numbing and not acknowledging my emotions at all. On my worst days, I did all the above including prayer. Ultimately, each person copes and heals using different approaches. Many times, multiple coping strategies prove to be more effective. This chapter shares my experiences and shines a light on how I found my rhythm in my healing journey. I did not have a manual, my faith was wavering, and my family and friends could not see my thoughts and insides to truly help. All I knew is, I wanted to be healed.

Pull It from the Root

In the midst of my brokenness, the closer I walked towards healing, the more broken I felt. As I was going through grief and loss, I realized how much I lost myself. There were times I just cried. Other times, I just stared off. I barely recognized myself. I didn't know If I was coming or going. I had begun to live without intent. I was free falling. Some days were like an outer body experience. Those days hurt the most because I was too broken to get up. Months and months passed by. I did not want to shop, travel, or have fun. I only wanted to work and sleep.

Several nights, I slept on the floor, too broken-hearted to sleep in the same bed that me and my past lover shared. Night after night, lying beside the bed on the floor, lifeless. It took about 8 months for me to realize how desolate and empty I was. The realization of how far I had fallen from what seemed like grace, made it hurt worse. I got tired of being my hurt self. I began meditating, walking, and praying more intensely. I even started going to therapy. My desire to be healed became so overwhelming, I started searching through every experience of loss and pain. I wanted to find the root cause of my true brokenness and what allowed me to stay in situations that no longer served me.

I wanted to uncover my own emptiness so I no longer relied on outsiders to fill my void. I recognize the importance of completing my own life and how relying on others would always lead to disappointment. Indeed, looking back and digging up old wounds began to hurt. Although it hurt my feelings, it fixed my vision. I began questioning my emptiness and lack of perspective. I stopped obsessing over my past and worrying about my future. It was hard work trying to be present in the moment. My new perspective helped me get to the root of my past failures and traumas. I realized some things were out of my control, and my past experiences had no power over my future. The choices I made shaped some of those negative experiences. There were stages and places where I stayed too long and other situations where I did not stay long enough.

Due to my lack of affection in my childhood, I held onto people, materials, and experiences past their expiration date. I realized how doing so hindered God from bringing new experiences into my life. In my introspection and deep digging, I, too, acknowledged how the pain was making me better. It was like the analogy of touching a hot flame. My neglect, pain, and disappointments were teaching me how to invest, who to love, and what to put my trust in. Some days, it was hard to look back. Other days, I couldn't force myself to look forward. It felt like looking forward was betraying my past.

I remembered a wise therapist saying, "You can't drive a car forward, looking in the rearview mirror." I learned it was okay to look back to reflect on lessons from the past but not to get stuck. Until I came to this realization, I was stuck, and far too long. By the grace of

God, I was overcoming. I needed to pull my trauma from the roots. I wanted to garden my life with wealth, happiness, and abundance. I couldn't do that, only tending to my surface wounds. I had to go deep. In doing so, I also found strength. My reflection not only showed me my flaws and bad choices, but they reminded me of my fight. I began to remind myself of the many trials and tribulations I overcame. The battle for my soul and mind was brutal. Slowing overcoming that battle was refreshing.

As it related to my failed relationships, few of them were not meant to be. I forced situations, lust, and affection on persons who were not for me. Some did not have the emotional maturity nor capacity to reciprocate what I had to offer. This was the same pattern for jobs and relationships. The only difference was, with jobs, I was compensated. With lust and betrayal, I had all the patience in the world. The things that were compensating me, I gave up easily. The situations and relationships that were draining me, I held onto for way too long. When I realized this, I got to the root of most of my issues. Day by day, I began to snatch it up.

Your Past is Dangerous

It was one year past what I would refer to as the most devastating heart-break of my life. I felt healed and happy that I was not where I used to be, but hurt that I wasn't fully where I should be. An epiphany came to me. I was going about my normal routine of breakfast and worship, when Sarah Jakes Roberts reminded me of my past. I had developed a routine to help expedite my healing. I needed a routine to help me be present and focused because my past seemed to still threaten my future.

Negative, intrusive thoughts haunted me daily. In this, I was afraid to move forward, and even more afraid to look back. My failed relationship triggered all my failures I had ever experienced. It made me begin to not only pick up my broken pieces, but start looking at each piece differently. I started analyzing the value of each broken piece and was careful about where I placed it in my life. I heard Sarah say, "Your past is dangerous!"

For a moment, I felt intimidated; but then I realized as she continued this was a good connotation. It was an oxymoron. She meant that my past had so much power, and yet, no power at all. The statement made me reflect on all the times I worked to heal past traumas and the challenges I had previously persevered through. At that moment, it came to me. This was just another season I had to reclaim my power. This was my season to take the wisdom from all my past experiences and transmute my pain into purpose.

The pain of my past meant finding the authentic me. Reflecting upon built-up disappointments, trauma, and disagreements that had gone unattended. Being broken down to my lowest was necessary for me to embrace a new beginning. My past was the key to my future success. My success was predicated on how I perceived my pain and what I decided to do with it. My previous negative perspective had my life in a free fall, a downward spiral. I found myself in a dark pit, wrestling with all the negative thoughts others had about me and the self-sabotaging thoughts I had about myself.

Depression had consumed so much of me. I no longer felt life was worth living. I lost my home and was less effective at my job. I struggled with ongoing rejection from people and situations. Truth is, those persons and situations were never for me. This new epiphany challenged my self-awareness. It made me reevaluate what I always knew to be true. Even worse, my self-esteem was impacted. I found out my perspective was flawed. The disappointment and the failures hurt, but they prepared me for the purpose. My past showed me where to place my energy. The pain and experiences taught me how to listen to my intuition and pay attention to the signs. In the midst of it all, I gained a heightened awareness. Pain taught me boundaries and emotional discipline. People that I would have normally trusted, I didn't. Situations I usually attached to, I kept at bay.

Along with purpose, I developed humility. I was rarely a boastful, prideful person. Though many times I was accused of being arrogant. I believed these accusations. Truth of the matter was, they didn't know how many trenches I had to climb out of to become the person I was. Success was far from easy for me. I survived hunger many days, homelessness at an early age, and also ongoing rejection due to my homosexual lifestyle. I grew up in a single-parent household with little to no income.

Many days, I came home with the lights disconnected and sometimes no water. In that, I had no desire to dumb down my success nor my blessings. To outsiders, I was arrogant. From my perspective, I was grateful. Even still, I learned grace. I stopped running from my past and started looking it directly in the face. This brought about new awareness, healing, and growth. I was able to capture wrong turns on my journey and also recognize how God made them work for my good. My spirituality grew. I became grounded in God and the promises he had for me. My past and my pain gave birth to my peace and my purpose. Once I transformed my perspective, I began to transform my life.

Fighting For Your Life

I fell asleep on my mom's couch the night before watching television. I can't remember what I was praying about but I do remember praying until I fell asleep. "Vegas!" my mom yelled from upstairs. "Yes ma'am?" I replied. The day before, her car had been repossessed, and she needed a ride to work. I didn't mind. Depression had led me to sleep on her too-small couch for two months. I was just getting to a place where I was present and living on purpose. I could feel my healing taking place. I was happy to slowly get back to myself. My mom hopped in my lifted Jeep Wrangler, grunting as she managed to get in. It was 8:32 a.m. I started my truck, and we headed out. My mom talked randomly as I drove her to work. It was normal for her to jump topics, but she did more when she was nervous or stressed out. She then asked, "You remember Sheila?" I thought for a moment and said, "Yes, what about her?". "Well, she is fighting for her life," my mom replied. She then turned and showed me a picture of a smashed vehicle where Ms. Sheila had been in a car accident. It looked like God stepped on the car himself. The car was unidentifiable. In that moment, I harbored in my spirit, "Thank you Jesus." I rushed to get my mom to work so she didn't see my tears fall. I pulled up in the round-about in front of her office and let her out. "Have a good day," she yelled as she wobbled to the glass door. I pulled off with cloudy eyes, and tears began to fall.

At that second I couldn't identify all the reasons I was crying.

I felt guilty about my days of complaining to God. I felt gratitude for how God kept me. I also felt confused about my future. What overwhelmed me the most, I looked back over all the things I had been through and remembered situations in that I wasn't supposed to survive. I could easily trace the favor of God over my life. This brought more tears to my eyes. I pulled over to the local county park and began thanking Jesus. I thanked him for the small things and blessings to come. I was at first worried about material things like vacations and which store would have a particular sneaker I wanted. Something about the statement "She is fighting for her life" struck me back to reality. Instantly, a spirit of gratitude filled me. After all, I had been through, my mind was in perfect peace, and my limbs and organs were operating perfectly. I also realized for the last 12 months, I, too, was fighting for my life. Depression whispered to me many days, "Give up and let go". The grace and presence of God kept me going. In retrospect, I could see how detrimental my fight could have been. Some people fight through trauma for their peace and mind, and still lose. Others persevere through accidents and domestic violence to save their own life.

In any circumstance, you have to fight for your life. Even if it's just a dream that seems as if it is never coming true. Sometimes, fighting requires forfeiting, and other times it demands a knock-out. The blessing in my new understanding of the fight was the realization that the ability to fight is a privilege in itself. Some people give up hope.

For me, I had to battle depression and struggle for my mind. A simple heartbreak triggered every trauma I ever experienced in my life. I fought like I never fought before. My fight required therapy, daily affirmations, exercising, manifestations, and spiritual growth.

On days I did not feel like I was winning, I cried and kept fighting. It required me to find a new strength I didn't know I possessed. I dug deep. Trauma taunted me with thoughts of suicide and fear of not being loved again. With prayer, and God, I fought. I am still fighting and grateful for my progression. I am more present than I have ever been, stronger than I have ever been. I value and appreciate the small nuances in life. The only thing on my need list is God. Gratitude is my new skin, and I am at peace. The things I lack, I understand that I am not supposed to have. What I have, it's my duty to keep. Fighting for my life, saved and transformed me.

The Waiting Room

After depression, life became so clear for me. I accepted that the past does not define the future. Acceptance helped the heartache and disappointment fade. Once I realized the affliction of others was not a reflection of me but a representation of who they were. Most importantly, I learned that growth comes with growing pains. My daily walks in the park became more peaceful. The stress from my job still persists, but I began to manage it with grace. Acceptance brought balance back into my life. Truth be told, God brought balance back into my life. I was sitting in the parking lot of the park meditating when I heard someone say, "You in the waiting room". It was a lady walking while talking on her cell phone. An epiphany came to me for no other reason than my own enlightenment. Life and emotions sometimes take us through an emergency. We tend to think our emergency is more urgent than others and rush to the hospital, where we find out there are people with more urgent matters than our own. We then wait in the waiting room to get seen. We show up with expectations to be seen, heard, and healed. Most times, we are seen, but our pain and concerns are not addressed. Other times, we are heard, but still not healed. More often than not, we get helped at the moment and sent home with the same ailments. I began to realize my own problems, worries, and ailments in life. I then understood the responsibility I had in my own healing process.

In any circumstance, a person seeking to be whole, happy, or healed must first communicate that they are hurt. It's almost impossible for doctors to address a need or a pain they have no clue about. A person must first acknowledge their own pain and need for help. Considering the waiting room, doctors and nurses do not randomly come to people. An ill person has to first reach out and communicate that they are not well. The ill person has to be willing to collaborate to get healed. Beyond this, the ill person has to be vulnerable enough to be fully transparent about the degree of their pain; or what they are willing to sacrifice to be healed. For example, a doctor may suggest cutting the limb off a diabetic to save the rest of the body. The doctor may view this as life-saving, whereas the patient may view this as a total loss of independence. Therefore, communicating a need for healing is only one step. Being open about the degree of pain is the second step. The most important step is understanding a sacrifice, and sometimes, a cutting must take place to save your life.

When patients arrive at the hospital, they check-in, discussing their reason for the visit. In triage, an initial screening takes place where the nurse asks, "On a scale of 1-10, how bad is your pain?" Depending on the results of that initial assessment, the patient is then placed in the waiting room, anticipating being seen and healed. For people that have been broken and hurting for a long time, the waiting room is the norm. Life begins to sometimes feel like a waiting room when your pain has gone unaddressed for so long. When you are hurting really bad, the wait seems longer. We sometimes get tempted to leave without treatment because it takes longer than expected. The realization is, that you can choose to be healed before you fully recover. Healing begins in the mind and in our choices. I realized I prolonged my own healing by choosing to stay in the waiting room. I sat there several years, instead of getting up and going to people and places that had the time and capacity to see me sooner. I had been spending time waiting for people that never had the time nor desire to help me. Even so, If they wanted to help, they did not have the capacity. I was accustomed to waiting and being broken.

Like others, the waiting room was my life, not even acknowledging that there were other doctors and other ways to get healed. I never accounted for other solutions, other people, or other opportunities that were within arm's reach and could have helped me achieve the healing and wholeness I was waiting for. I realized healing was a choice. We can sit and wait in the waiting room for someone to call us or see us while gambling is being misdiagnosed or dismissed. Alternatively, we can take the necessary steps towards our own healing, even while waiting. Being in a waiting room is a good start, but when you get there you have to be vulnerable and desperate enough to get healed. You have to expose your brokenness sometimes to strangers and be willing to be embarrassed and release your ego in order to be acknowledged faster. Being ill and needing healing is not enough; you have to desire to be active in your own healing process. The waiting room is the neutral place between broken and healed. You can stay broken because it's taking too long, or you can irritate the doctors until they see you. This is the same concept as faith and God. Needing a miracle and waiting for one is not enough. You have to be desperate enough to demand a miracle through faith. Prayer is not enough, you have to pray and believe.

Go Through It

I remember my life being simple. I went to work, I paid my bills, and I came home. In the midst of my pain and healing, I began to get closer to God, and things began to change. Ironically, life became more chaotic. My job became more stressful and even discriminatory. I applied for promotions that I was more than qualified for and was denied. Outside of work, it was good chaos, but all times unpredictable. I started meditating, and praying. Some days, I walked in the park and made quiet time for myself. The more I did these things, the more my life began to shift. It seemed like everything was falling apart but together at the same time. I started analyzing my surroundings and the people in it. My desire to eliminate empty experiences and purposeless people began to grow. At the same time, it seemed as if everything was against me. My leaders at work would call it "imposter syndrome". This of course, was to project onto me their guilt of discriminating and rejecting me. I wondered why I should pray if the results seem to not progress. This random day, the answer came to me. I had been hearing it in my spirit all along. "Go through it. Keep pushing", something on the inside would say. God was taking me through challenges to qualify me for who he ultimately knew I would become. Without those experiences, I would not excel at being that person.

Most of the experiences were experiences I thought I initiated myself. Sadly, I was wrong. I was in the season of learning and realized that nothing was by mistake. Even the bad experiences were working together for my good. It took me 33 years of life to recognize this. My next level of dimension required me to be broken, blind, and lost. I had to be broken enough to look inside and desire healing and purpose. When I looked back, I saw pain, but I also saw miracles. God had taken my mistakes and turned them into lessons. I was able to acknowledge my choice pattern and derive the good from the bad. It became clear to me how and where I got lost and the distractions that normally led me bewildered.

Most importantly, I recognize how the grace of God was constantly bestowed upon my life. God kept me even in the midst of my disgrace, stupidity, redundancy, and toxic cycles. My reflection became my inflection. My inflection helped me identify my infection. I learned accountability. Before I knew it, transformation began to set in. More and more, my perspective began to change. I felt lighter and started to think differently. I changed, but also stayed the same. My view on challenges shifted. I learned that resisting the pain and trauma only prolonged it. You cannot heal what is covered up. I started to peel back the layers and grew a greater appreciation for the pain and how it was developing my character. I realized that if I survived my past, I could overcome anything. With my improved outlook, I began to get my fight and hope back.

Chapter 3
Embrace It

The moment I acknowledged my trauma and began to work through it, I began to find peace again. Even more healing, I began to find myself. Self-actualization began to take place for me in new ways. Self-actualization is defined as the realization or fulfillment of one's potential and/or talents. Healing helped open up new methods of expression and creativity. I stopped perceiving my pain and past an embarrassment and instead a testimony. I embraced each disappointment, heartbreak, and failure as an opportunity to grow. I changed the narrative in my mind about failure. This was the most monumental action that thrust my healing forward. Trauma and pain only have the power a person gives it. Ruminating in hurt, grief, and disappointment gives the pain and trauma the dictation over your future. I became familiar with the art of alchemy. Alchemy is the study and act of transmuting negative energy and experiences into positive outcomes. I retrained my mind to view each negative experience as a vehicle to develop my adaptability skills. My journey and my spirit became lighter. I embraced each challenge, and as a result, accepting change was easier. I practiced gratitude for the small things in life, which helped comfort my soul. The areas I experienced lack, I compensated in the areas I was abundant. When I didn't have money, I was grateful for peace. When my peace was not intact, I was grateful to have faith.

A Refill

Freedom started to ring in my spirit as the wind caressed my skin. I felt myself coming back. My faith and hope began growing again from within me. My focus was no longer on the past. I became filled with gratitude and no longer obsessed over situations that did not work out. It was a reminder to my spirit of God's divine timing and purpose for my life. My perspective on closed doors and rejection shifted. I began to accept that rejection was sometimes protection. I gained clarity on how my past relationships not working out was a distraction to my destiny. If I continued to focus on the pain, rejection, and lack of reciprocity, I would never reach where and who I was truly destined to be. Since I Shifted my perspective, it allowed for a new chapter in my life. This new chapter highlighted closed doors and rejection as redirection. I gained the ability to heal from disappointment and hurt faster, even better, not be hurt at all. Rejection no longer impacted my self-esteem or self-awareness. I considered failed plans as plans that were absent from God's plan. Acceptance became my new skin. My pores opened back up to life. My spirit felt rejuvenated. I could tell my troubling days were coming to an end. I could feel God about to thrust me into a new dimension of love, life, and peace.

Cease the Search

A flashback came to my mind. I was laying in the Motel 6 bedroom, room 207, where I had been staying since I lost my home. Out of nowhere, I started thinking about how broken I was in the past. My mind rewinded the heartbreak, and I could see how lost I had been in previous months. It was like an outer body experience, looking back at someone else. I was able to reflect on how grief and depression had me so bound, I couldn't see myself. I was searching and looking for answers in places I had never looked before. Reflecting, I could do nothing but continuously thank God for how he kept me during those times.

I was most grateful that during my times of depression and desolation, I did not turn to drugs and alcohol. The environment you are in during times of brokenness is important. It can determine whether you emerge healed and wiser or trapped in addiction and resentment. The wrong environment can convert a temporary stage of grief into a lifelong addiction and self-sabotaging behaviors. I knew it was God that kept me far from those extremes. As broken and hurt as I was, I didn't have the desire to do drugs. I knew I was closer than I had ever been to losing me. I needed me. Others and my family needed me. I remember being so lost and confused, that I reached out to several psychics, spending money month after month looking for answers. I didn't understand why my relationship did not work out. I was questioning if God truly loved me and if he was truly for me.

In one instance, I was so intrigued and comforted by the answers, I ended up paying $350 for a reading. Part of it was my rent money. At that moment, she provided me with the comfort and clarity that I had been searching for months for. It was a temporary relief, but in my perspective, worth every penny. My brokenness made me dabble in different religions and practices, trying to accommodate the pain and the questions. Though I was searching, I wasn't lost enough to believe I didn't need God at all. I interpreted different perspectives and combined them with my traditions. This gave me my own understanding and unique relationship with God. New revelations about who I was and who God was for me came to me. On days I thought I could not breathe, I still knew God was the reason I had to breathe. Practices such as tarot readings, sound healing, and reiki became attractive to me. These new concepts helped me get instant comfort from my pain. I knew God would prevail, still, but I was too hurt to wait. Daily horoscopes helped me walk my healing journey, one day at a time. At times, this backfired. Some horoscope predictions proved to be true as they related to my pain.

Other times, it validated my faith and belief in God's plan to renew me and give me more than I could ever imagine. Though these tactics gave me hope, the generalizations of tarot and horoscopes did not speak directly to my circumstances. At moments, they came close, but over time lost the truth. I needed to experience that. I needed to be reminded in my soul that God had the final say so and the true answers my soul was longing for. This helped me to cease the search. Finding a way to quiet all the outside voices and perspectives, guided me back to my truth. Clarity started to seep in. Daily affirmations and prayer brought peace back into my life. I began to understand the phrase "peace that surpasses all understanding".

For decades, I didn't understand. Most days, I was financially broke, sleeping on my mama's couch, where depression led me. Despite this, I had peace in my heart. I knew it had to be God's grace. I realized that it had only been 3 months prior that I was so depressed, I was borderline suicidal. I still had a nice job, two homes, and a decent amount of money, but I was still lost and torn. My morals began to change. Materials no longer fascinated me. New shoes and going to every party no longer amused me. I found joy in sitting in the park, watching the ripple of the lake. Working out at the gym made me feel empowered, something I had never done outside of school sports. A simple $1.89 sundae from McDonalds made my day. My search for peace was over. I could feel the joy of my soul starting to leap again. I was overwhelmed. I knew I had been born again.

A Breath of Fresh Wind

Acceptance is what sets me free. I began to accept the misfortunes and disappointments as part of life. The less I tried to control every outcome in my life, the less anxious and stressed I was. I surrendered to the divine and, most importantly, God. I knew that if God allowed it, he would also find a way to use it for my good. I began living for one day at a time, daring not to look back. When I was tempted to look back, I reminded myself that driving forward while looking in the rearview mirror would lead to a crash. My life began to progress with peace. My pain and problems had not yet disappeared, but my perspective on them had changed. I no longer let issues I could not control impact my joy. I felt the grace of God fall over me. I was connected to myself and the world again. Many days were challenging, but I pushed through. Simply getting out of the bed or off the floor, no longer seemed impossible. I began to get excited about what my future held. Each day, I manifested joy and peace. Life seemed so free. The things I used to obsess and worry about, became a joke. I knew my destiny lied in God's hands.

Diamond in the Ashes

In the midst of picking up the pieces, I noticed a flickering in the dust. The gravel, for a moment, had me distracted. I was unable to identify what it was. Looking closer, it was clear like crystal. My curiosity kicked in. It was a new hope. My hope for living and life began appearing even in the darkness. I knew God, and my angels heard my prayers. I thought my past would keep me bound and lost. The flickering, like other things, showed me otherwise. My daily walks, affirmations, and prayers began taking route in my heart. My mind sometimes still challenged my faith, but the flickering of new opportunities and new beginnings helped me refocus. No longer did I internalize my circumstances as failure and punishment. I knew a closed door meant another door was opening. Each door that opened, I went in, praying that God would show me what was for me.

A Prayer Money Can't Buy

In the midst of healing from heartbreak and depression, so many lessons were bestowed upon me. The best part of my healing journey was getting back to myself. Even more rewarding, I gained wisdom along the way. Materialistic and financial gain had little value to me. Indeed, I still wanted both, but not having neither did not leave me empty. I remember days I was so hurt and broken, I would just pray for peace and the strength to not lose my mind. So many others who experienced the same degree of pain and betrayal did not come out as healthy and stable as myself. I thanked God. Gratitude 80became my new smile. I thought about my cousin, who was more like my sister. We were raised in the same house for several years. She was six years older than me. In her childhood, she had experienced so much pain, neglect, and sexual abuse. She wore the pain in her life. Drugs became my cousin's way of coping, and addiction set in. At first, she would get pissy drunk. I mean literally drank until she peed her clothes. At that time, she was only 17-18 years old. This was her onset, and cried out for help. My family ignored it. My other cousins and I were too young to understand or identify this. We thought it was funny. Her addiction progressed. She began using cocaine. At first, she was ashamed and would lie about it or hide the fact that she used it.

Eventually, she became so comfortable, that it was not strange for her to pull out a sandwich bag full of powder and snort it off her pinky right in your presence. Not many years afterward, rumors began to circulate that she was using 'crack,' casting a shadow over her once-promising future. I remember the news piercing my heart like an arrow. Seeing her made me break down, but it also made me thank God. I knew I, too, had enough pain and troubles to run me to drugs, but since he kept me and covered me, I only had a taste for wholeness and healing. I also understood that if she wanted, God would heal her and bind her addiction as well. The only difference was, I asked and desired to be healed. My understanding of this gave me little comfort about my cousin's situation. I knew when she truly wanted to be free, God would set her free. I still prayed for her. I prayed for several reasons; mainly giving thanks for the provision and protection over my life. Even more importantly, giving God thanks for keeping her alive and well even in the midst of addiction and life-altering drugs. When I saw others in pain, it instantly reminded me how close I was to losing my mind. God and my mama's couch saved me. Most days, my pockets were full of money, but my mind was at peace, and my heart was empty. It was at a point that money could not do anything for me. I needed God. I needed healing and answers that money could not buy. My heart longed for truth. The more I prayed, the more I discovered. Some nights, I cried and prayed until I was sound asleep. Other nights, I couldn't say a word. I knew God could hear the whispers in my heart. I could feel he did.

Not Settling For Safe

It was 4:45 a.m. The alarm clock sounded. My body was exhausted. I slapped the alarm clock like a fly on my grandma's wall. It was one of those days, I wanted to give up. I lay in the Motel 6 bed, thinking of 30 reasons why I shouldn't give up. I thought about all my losses. The enemy tried every trick he could with my mind. I managed to force myself out of bed. I hopped in the shower and let the hot water scorch over my body. Normally, lukewarm water would have been my preference, but in this case wanted to clean off my feelings of despair. I hurried up to not be late for work. I clocked in just in time. My mind raced, wondering what I would tell my boss, considering I needed to leave work early. I had been waiting all week for this day.

At noon, I was scheduled to go to a casting call. Acting and being a musician was always a dream for me. I had recently been accepted by a modeling and casting agency for beginners in the industry. It was only my third casting call; the first one paid. I was conflicted on whether to stay at work or jump out on faith and give my dreams one last shot. .The role was only paying $50.00. I needed money, but I needed to respark my dreams and hope even more. I worked 5 hours and decided I'd put in PTO. I knew I was still taking a risk, considering my boss was controlling and ran the job like a slave plantation. It was presented as a lack of accountability, but the truth is, corporate companies like control. My mind and thought tried to convince me to back out but I knew I had been playing it safe far too long. I realized all the opportunities I let pass me by because I feared losing a job I hated anyway. I turned off my work phone and clocked out. Call time for the casting call was at 12:00 p.m. I hurried back to the hotel room to change and shower, then rushed out the door. I jumped in my jeep and headed for Crowders Mountain.

When I arrived, the parking lot seemed empty. I parked and began to walk around what looked like a campground. "Excuse me!" I yelled across the gravel to a random lady. "Can you tell me where the casting call for the movie is?" I asked. She pointed to a large loft uphill. I walked up the slope of rocks to a gazebo where two people stood. "Hello", the lady greeted me saying. "Hi!" I replied excitedly. "I am here to sign in for the casting call," I assured her. She swabbed my nostrils with a thin white cotton swab to test for COVID-19. I squeezed my eyes tight. Each time I thought we were over the Covid pandemic, a random swab brought me back to reality. "Okay, everyone is waiting in the lodge," she pointed. I began to pray and walk. It was 80 degrees, and I was dressed like a cowboy. When I arrived, people were scrambling like roaches. It instantly boosted my morale. This was a real casting call, nothing like the others I had been to. Wardrobe staff were moving fast with wardrobe carts, make-up artists were off in the corners doing touch-ups, and hair stylists were spraying other actresses' hair. I walked to the side that was as empty as possible to read the room better. Reading the room, I realized how much I stood out. Everyone was there to play a role in the movie. "Listen up! If you have not seen the make-up artist or have gotten your wardrobe approved, please let me know," a guy wearing a headset yelled. At that moment, it hit me. I was in a room of potential millionaires. I began to praise God in my spirit. Something defining in that moment helped me realize how close my dreams were. "Hey. My name is Shar", I said to the guy across the table from me. Everyone in the room was dressed as country music fans. "I'm Mark", he replied. He was an older, white male appearing to be introverted and business savvy. I became curious about his background and what landed him in the room. "So, are you from this area?" I asked. "No, I'm from Kentucky. I am actually retired and decided I'd respond to an Ad for cast. I am retired from the banking industry," he continued. "Hmm. It's a very good time to retire from banking", I sarcastically replied. We both laughed. "Everyone, please complete your w9 forms, and get ready. We will be heading to the barn shortly," the man with the headset yelled. I continued to read the room. With each scan, it became more real to me. I was on my first real set. I realized that this day had the potential to change my life forever.

Butterflies Do Not hang with Caterpillars

I was sitting in my vehicle one day after work in reflection. I was reflecting on my life and the paths I decided to take. That day, like many, I had an inquisitive spirit. I was healing and in a better place. I was still going through retaliation and discrimination at work, but I made the decision not to let it hinder me. I was healing and in a better place than I had been in a while. Emotionally, I still had a way to go. I remember watching a YouTube video, and the concept of transformation came to mind. The narrator mentioned caterpillars and their transitional stage into becoming a butterfly. It was at that moment that clarity came to me. The areas of my life that were stuck and non-progressive were those I attempted to fit in instead of standing out. This created more resistance in my process of growth. I began to accept and understand that transformation happens over time and through experiences. I failed to realize the most subtle times of transformation and therefore missed the "turn signal". Turn signals are clues that God and the universe provide to us, even without us asking. Sometimes, those signals come in the form of adversity, other times, they show up as miracles and blessings. I missed several signals, too caught up in my pain and past. It became clear to me that I was a butterfly, still longing to crawl around with caterpillars. This longing stemmed from familiarity and comfort zone. Because we shared the same background, I rejected the idea of neglecting what was familiar to me. A sense of betrayal plagued me each time I wanted to fly away.

When I wanted to change my job, or relocate my home, I subconsciously checked the rearview mirror. I also referred back to my cultural norms and surroundings. This did not help my ability to accept change. My intentions were to keep myself grounded, but I truly kept myself stagnant. Although I started as a caterpillar, becoming a butterfly came with new abilities, new visions, and new heights. I could no longer crawl on the ground or hide in a cocoon. My wings were expanded and ached to be set free. Even though I was related to the caterpillar, it was no longer my path. I recall the YouTube video describing caterpillars attempting to leave the cocoon too soon or stay too long.

The narrator discussed the possibility of death if a butterfly attempts to stay in a cocoon longer than intended. This was clarifying for me. I began to understand why living a routined, mediocre life caused me internal turmoil. I had butterfly dreams, crawling around to caterpillar expectations. It hurt. I was suffocating my dreams and abilities. I began to realize some relationships and my job no longer felt comfortable. I had outgrown those people and environments. I was prolonging the process of moving forward due to comfort. The lessons that each person and each environment was intended to show me were also proposed to elevate me. Once I elevated my thought process, the physical comfort of staying in the relationship or staying at the job no longer served me. I learned my biggest mistake of the past and mistakes others make all the time; staying past my purpose.

Awareness helped shift my perspective about my life. Each day, I woke up, still doing mediocre tasks, but also executing plans to help me fly. My family and friends considered me impulsive. I began taking risks that most everyday people would not take. As I slowly transformed my body, I also transformed my mind. I stop giving my energy to small-minded people. I stopped sharing my dreams with people who lacked ambition. I limited the access to me to decrease as much negative influence in my life as possible. My spirit got lighter, and my mind became clear. I was able to set my intentions and move forward in my life.

The Room is Ready

I was sitting in the parking lot of the local library, where I normally went to research and write. All of a sudden, I noticed a man sleeping under a tree. The weather was 30 degrees outside. It instantly struck my heart. What hurt most, I had nothing to offer him. For some, this would have been a normal thing. As for me, I remembered all the times I was desolate, cold, and alone. I remembered how my faith began to waiver during those times, and I began questioning God. Not for long, did the spirit not remind me that it was also God who kept my mind in perfect peace during those times. I began to cry and rejoice with thanksgiving. When I looked back at how depressed I was and how many days suicidal thoughts lived rent-free in my head, I knew it had to be something bigger than me that brought me out. A sense of gratitude began to fill my heart. Tears ran down my eyes. I prayed and cried, thanking God for every storm he brought so I could appreciate the sunshine.

Looking at the man sleeping on the ground in the cold was like looking back at my old self. After a few moments, I gathered my belongings and headed inside the library. "Do you have a study room available?" I asked the librarian. "Not at this moment, but I can go and ask the previous person to leave," she replied. The library allowed each person to use a private study room for two hours daily. Once the two hours were up, you could stay until someone else requests to use the room. "No problem. I'll just sit over here in the corner until they leave." I replied. Moments later, I heard the librarian say, "Ms. Moore, the room is ready for you". At that moment, chills began to run down my spine. Although she was talking about a small study room in a public library, her statement echoed in my spirit. I remembered the promise of God and how he stated he would prepare a table for me, before my enemies. I had a flashback on how long life had me waiting for a room, a blessing, an acknowledgement, and a promise to be ready for me. She had no clue about the confirmation she gave me when she made the statement. The librarian and I walked around the corner to the available study room. It was well-lit. The room was a boardroom with 8 seats and a large table. Behind me was a 50-inch flat screen. "Do you have everything you need?" she asked. "Yes!" I replied. I closed the door behind me and rightfully took my seat at the head of the table. In that instance, I knew God wanted me to begin practicing and visualizing what the table and the room would be like. I heard in my spirit, "You are the head and not the tail, and every room you walk in from here on out, I will prepare before you." I could not resist rejoicing. Life showed me that divine timing is better than my own. Even a good thing at the wrong time is still a bad thing. Receiving a blessing, a job, or a relationship too soon could mean losing it as soon as you receive it. I was grateful God allowed me to know he was preparing situations, circumstances, and rooms before me. I was a fool and had proved so many times. In my experiences, I learned the importance as well as the difference between man's preparation and God's preparation. The differences were far and between. Like a baby, when we think we are prepared, we go through circumstances prematurely. In doing so, our growth and development is stunted. We then need additional nurturing, additional attention, extra care, and a special kind of love. Most times, we are in the wrong places and around the wrong people to receive such. When God prepares a room or a thing, we won't long for people and places that do not have the capacity to fill us. I used to think they did not have the love nor the desire, but time and time again, I figured out capacity and integrity are way more important.

Filled to Capacity

I was in Houston, TX hanging out on the rooftop bar with friends. We laughed and had a few drinks, and decided to leave and get something from a local Mexican restaurant. It was a Saturday night, and the bar and every business around it was busy. My friends and I stepped into the hall to wait on the elevator to get to our vehicles. Several elevators came, but they quickly filled up. Eventually, we heard "ding!". Finally, an empty elevator. My friends and I, along with several others who had been waiting, crammed in the elevator. We went from the 13th floor down to the 11th floor when the elevator door opened.

People were standing, looking to see if we had room to allow them in. The elevator was packed. We closed the door to proceed down to the first floor. Before we could get down, the elevator stopped and opened again on the 5th floor. Again, people standing on the outside peered in, hoping they could fit in. We were filled to capacity. I could see the look on their faces each time we stopped, and they realized that it was not yet their time. Even worse, we were beginning to get frustrated with the packed elevator and wanted to get to the first floor. Covid-19, a deadly disease, had not long devastated the entire world, and so people were not yet comfortable being in close proximity for so long. I know I wasn't. We finally reached the first floor and burst out the elevator doors like a cracked can of biscuits. People began to move like ants with relief. In what felt like a forever experience, I realized the importance of capacity. The elevator engineers early on had established a weight limit and person capacity for each elevator for safety. Any time the elevator was overloaded and had too many riders, it posed a risk. If over capacity, the elevator could break down and experience mechanical failure. As humans, we are much like elevators. Life takes us through experiences and relationships in stages, better yet, levels. With each level we experience different people and challenges that may enter our lives. Sometimes, we are stopped at levels or circumstances we had no intentions on stopping at. In these encounters, we have a choice. We can allow that moment to hinder our final destination, or we can overlook the setback and keep going. More importantly, we have the responsibility of knowing our capacity. See, an elevator does not know its capacity until it's too late. Sometimes, as humans, we operate in the same manner. We take on burden after burden, heartbreak after heartbreak, and keep on going, never stopping to check our capacity.

The single mother takes care of the home, the children, work, and sometimes other family members. The overworked father takes on the bills, the responsibility of the car, being a provider and protector, and the societal pressure of always having to be strong. The teenager has the responsibility of finding out who they are while being pressured to be someone else, succeeding in school, childhood traumas, and the inclination to make their parents proud. The list of responsibilities goes on and on. Rarely, do we stop and check our capacity. When most people realize they are at capacity, like the elevator, it's too late. You have already broken down, already had a mental break or a heart attack.

More commonly, you have already neglected the child, neglected the spouse, or even worse, neglected yourself. This is why recognizing your own capacity is important. If you do not know how much you can take, you have no clue how much you can give. Knowing your own capacity means learning when to say "no" and when to let go. This includes people: relationships, situations, jobs, grief, and disappointments. It's easier to recognize capacity in others because it does not require us to look at ourselves. I learned that knowing my own capacity helped me understand when someone else was at their capacity. Understanding this helped me to not require of people what they could not give me. Sometimes, we require loyalty, love, understanding, and attention from people who do not have the capacity to give them to us. If we do not understand capacity, this leads to disappointment after disappointment, sometimes affecting our self-esteem because we think something is wrong with us. In truth, that person does not have mental or emotional room to love us, to be loyal, or have concern. Most times, it is not personal nor intensional, it's lack of capacity. This does not take away the guilt or that person's responsibility to recognize their own capacity and have integrity, but it does offer perspective. How can you give what you don't know you have?

My Peace is Not for Sale

My alarm clock sounded. I heard the geese quacking outside. I remembered I was in Durham, North Carolina, where God gave me a new start and a new career path. Truth be told, part of my healing journey was to let go of everything old and start new. I decided to walk away from my old job that was emotionally and mentally abusing me. I also decided to relocate to a new city I had no recollection of trauma nor pain in. I was previously burned out from leading and working with so many others in the mental health field and retail. I decided to relocate for a HVAC technician program; a trade I had taken up in the midst of my pain to help keep my mind sane. The relocation and the job I was not totally sure about, but my insides were screaming for new. My new supervisor was the typical older male. He was African American and from the era where women were inferior to men. I could tell he was not fond of working alongside women, but he could tell I was not the typical woman. It was getting closer to my 90 day probationary period. I had been working for almost $5 less per hour than I was used to. I knew I would have to learn more skills in the field so I accepted the pay cut. I also was receiving monthly bonuses and a 2 bedroom home at a discount. Most days were smooth. Other days, I found myself picking up trash near the dumpsters in total shock. Those were the days I felt like I fell from grace. What I didn't realize was my job description as an HVAC Service Technician included waste management, janitorial services, and anything else my manager thought of. The endurance and perseverance in me would not let me quit. The ambition in me would not let me stay in peace. Here I was a college graduate with a B.A. in Criminal Justice and 48 hours completed of a 60 credit hours M.A. in Clinical Mental Health, at a dumpster chasing squirrels away from trash. Some days were worse. Many times I found myself in cat urine filled apartments, under the kitchen cabinet with roaches trying to fix a 10 year old garbage disposal. With each spin of my drill, I questioned God. It had been a long day of dirty toilets and AC repairs. My supervisor was doing his usual demeaning things, such as asking me to go clean doggie bins near the doggie park. Apparently it was part of my job description but he only mentioned it when he felt I was questioning his authority. Truly I was challenging his integrity because it was clear he did not have any. To his surprise, I ran off and cleaned the doggie bins with a smile. I walked into the leasing office where the office personnel worked. The assistant manager looked at me and said "Are you okay? You seem to be dragging." I was tired but didn't realize it was that apparent. I replied, "I'm just tired". She continued by saying "Well I would milk the clock because now you are in overtime and will get the money you deserve." She didn't realize it but it struck me. My first thought was, "so you guys know my worth but refuse to pay it?". My former thought was "It ain't worth my peace". I looked back at her and replied, "There is not a dollar you can pay me for my peace". She was taken back but in agreement. Here I was a 35 year old telling her at age 63 that it was more to life than money. No matter how good the money seems, if it's costing you your health or peace, then it's costing you more to make it than its paying you to keep it. Although I had the words and wisdom, a flashback of my life came over me. I began to recall times I sold myself short; in relationships, on jobs, and friendships. A spirit of grief entered my heart. I began to ask myself why. "What makes you continue to invest where there is no return?" "What make you stay where you are not welcomed?" The answer was overwhelming. It was my childhood trauma. I grew up in a single parent household. My mother worked late nights and I was without a father figure for several years. When I finally embraced my mother's boyfriends as a father figure, most of the damage was already done. My mother did not have time to do murturing or motherly things like cook or atttend my sports games. My father did, but I always had to live with the thought that he was not my real father. When he introduced me to his real family and friends as his daughter, I remember the look on their faces. I didn't realize it as a child, but in retrospect, I was neglected. In actuality, I was neglected in the worst way; emotionally. From as early as 8 years old, I fell in love with rejection. Due to my childhood, I was accustomed to being alone; physically and emotionally. When my stepfather dropped me off home, he dropped me off to an empty house and told me lock the door. Since my mom worked at night and I was in school during the day, I sometimes did not see my mom for days at a time. This created a longing to be loved and accepted by others. Luckily, this did not manifest in my childhood as violence, drug use, or teenage pregnancy. That longing carried over into my adulthood and relationships. I fell into patterns of loving people who did not love me and trying to prove my worthiness of their love. I invested in situations that did not benefit me or have a return on my investment. I jeopardized my peace for others' presence. After several heartbreaks and disappointments, I found acceptance. It required me to look at my wounds and trace down my pain. The little neglected girl was still showing up in my adulthood. When I sat down with her, acknowledged her, and healed her, I became free. I no longer desire to be in the company or places where I am not welcomed. I do not long for attention nor love that is not freely given to me. I appreciate solitude and alone time to nurture myself. I rely on self love to heal and make me happy. Most importantly, I became me.

About The Author

Shar Vegas Moore was born on July 8, 1989, in Columbia, South Carolina. Her mother, Jennifer Moore, was born in Long Island, New York, and was raised in Detroit, Michigan, by adoptive parents. After moving from Detroit, Jennifer Moore met SharVegas' father and later gave birth to the author in Columbia, SC.

Shar grew up in a single-parent home with her mother as her primary parent. Being the only child, oftentimes, her cousins were referred to as siblings. From elementary school through high school, the author found comfort in writing and emotional expression through poetry and music. As an introvert, the need to express developed a deeper passion for writing. The author continued to write literary content such as poetry and short stories at the age of 11. With literary influences such as Maya Angelou, Richard Wright, and Langston Hughes, she began to polish her craft through writer's workshops and accepting opportunities to create literature as often as possible.

Shar continued to write music and literature throughout high school and college. She first began receiving public recognition for her work at her 8th-grade graduation. Her Poem was published as part of the graduation program and recited live by the young author. Attending Edward Waters College in Jacksonville, FL., was a transition from a small rural city to a large urban area. This allowed the author to expand her writings to become more diverse. Learning new cultures and ways of life through the exploitation of life help expand her creative content. In 2016, the author published her first book, "The Conscious Collection". The book was published on all major platforms globally, including Amazon, Barnes & Nobles. In 2018, the author began to receive recognition from the community and was inducted into the local author's spotlight in public libraries in South Carolina and North Carolina. Her work was later added to the public library catalog made available to the community.

As a Certified Life Coach, Behavior Technician, Mental Health Professional and youth advocate, the author extended her works to include children's books. In 2021, Shar released her first children's book "Be Yourself" through LuLu Publishing. Her motivation for publishing the work was to inspire minority youth and youth of LGBTQ backgrounds to embrace their differences. Later, moving to Miami, FL, after graduating college was an eye-opener for the young author. She began to learn about the environment and the importance of "self-awareness." With the value of "self" came the acceptance of "differences." Financial hardship and life-changing events drove the young author to be even more motivated to succeed and influence others. Committed to giving back, she immediately became active in the local non-profit in her community. Fulfilled with fostering the academic success of other low-income youth, she extended her non-profit efforts of her newly incorporated Motivated Hearts Foundation Inc., from Miami, FL, to include Columbia, SC, as well. In the opinion of the author, community service is a huge part of her success and ability to persevere through everyday challenges. In 2023, Shar published "Use Your Voice!" A children's book to help youth identify healthy touching and sexual assault at the early onset. Doing so was important to the other as she encountered several sexual assault victims working with youth through her nonprofit efforts. As the author continues to write, she aspires to impact the world through literature. Her versatility and multi-faucet background bring value to different genres. Her style of deliverance and ability to capture an audience is what is bound to make her an Amazon Bestseller and world-renowned author.

Made in the USA
Middletown, DE
22 July 2024

57625083R00046